# Matchstick Mini celebrate Patrick's Day

# By Edel Malone

Original concept created, illustrated, and written by Edel Malone. I'm sure you will love these books as much as I do. I know you will enjoy making lasting memories with your child moving forward in all stages of their lives by encouraging your child to tell you what's on their mind throughout their lifetime. Asking questions is the way forward. Check out some of the other Matchstick Mini books. Sizes and colors may vary for printed books.

The Matchstick Mini books are designed to encourage your child to open up and talk about what is on their mind from an early age. The topics covered are related to young children to encourage good communication techniques carrying on into each stage of their lives, keeping safety and values in mind.

# OTHER BOOKS FROM MATCHSTICK MINI

Matchstick Mini and safety

Matchstick Mini and others

Matchstick Mini has fun

Matchstick Mini and school

Matchstick Mini is very good

Matchstick Mini is healthy

Matchstick Mini and grief

Matchstick Mini loves celebrating St. Patrick's Day because it is only once a year. He always wears green to celebrate St. Patrick's Day and has lots of fun. Matchstick Mini and his little sister make green flags to bring to the parade to celebrate St. Patrick's Day with their family.

Matchstick Mini uses face paint to draw green shamrocks on his face, and his little sister does too. They always bring their green flags to wave on St. Patrick's Day and they love to watch the parade.

Matchstick Mini and his little sister love going to the parade to watch all the different floats and bands going along in the parade, and they love to see all the other people dressed in green. Do you like to celebrate St. Patrick's Day like Matchstick Mini and his little sister?

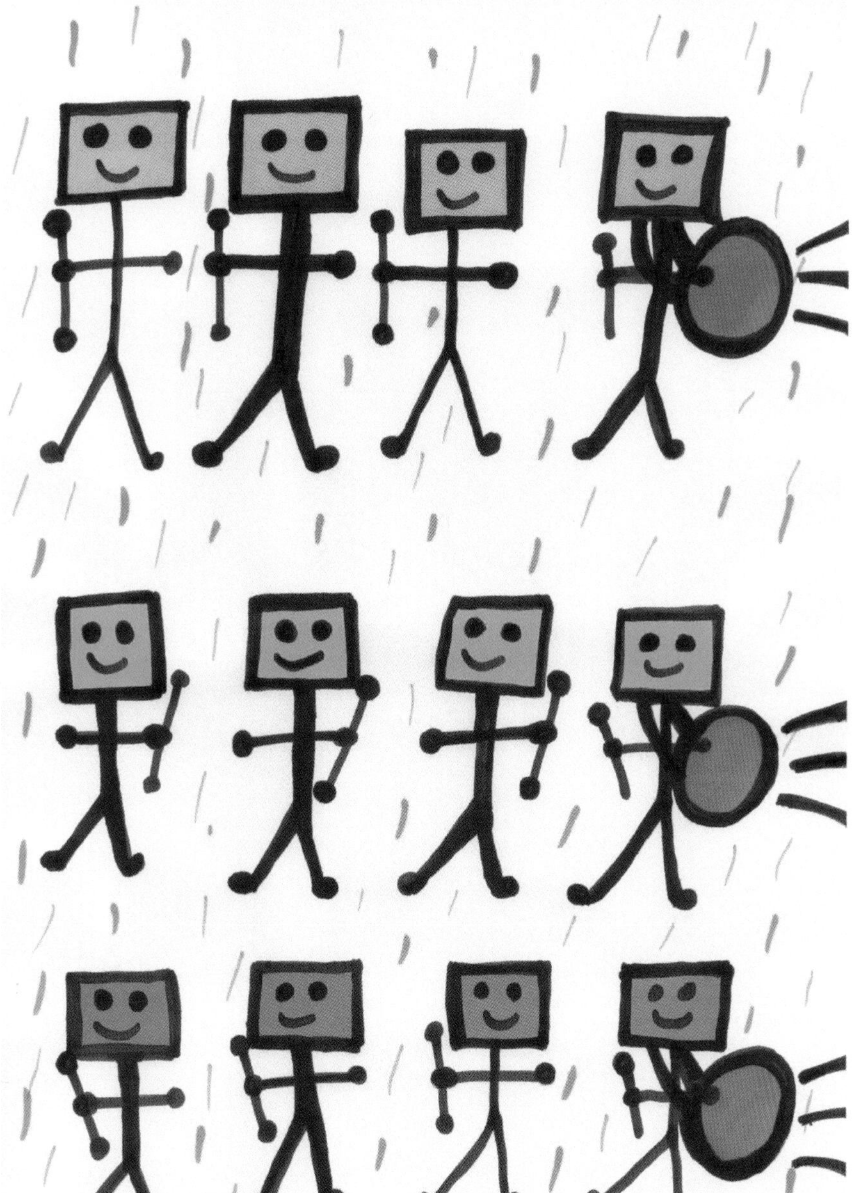

Matchstick Mini and his little sister love waving their flags, and they are excited to see lots of other people dressed up waving their flags too. When Matchstick Mini looks across the road and sees all the other people waving flags, he thinks it looks like a giant sea of green.

Matchstick Mini loves all the different costumes, uniforms and traditional clothes from around the world. There are so many people from other countries, and he loves that people from other countries come to celebrate St. Patrick's Day wearing their traditional clothes. Matchstick Mini loves to see new things and learn about other people's traditions and loves to watch people from other countries performing in the parade.

Matchstick Mini loves to watch all the dancing groups in the parade. All the dancing groups are doing lots of different types of dancing. There are Irish dancers, hip hop dancers, tap dancers, so many other types of dancers. Matchstick Mini loves dancing, and he loves to watch other people dancing too. Matchstick Mini loves going to his dance classes and taking part in dancing competitions too.

There are people dressed up as clowns handing out sweets and balloons at the parade, and when the clowns give Matchstick Mini and his little sister some sweets, they say thank you to the clowns. The clowns beep their horns, splash people with water, and give some other children some sweets and balloons too. Matchstick Mini and his sister think the clowns are funny and everyone has a great day at the parade.

Matchstick Mini and his little sister see street performers on funny bicycles going by, and some of these bikes have only one wheel, and some have three wheels. Matchstick Mini's little sister laughs because she thinks the bikes look very funny, and she wonders if she could cycle a bike with only one wheel. Matchstick Mini and his family always stay together on a day out, so no one gets lost. Matchstick Mini and his family are very clever. Do you always stay near adults on a day out like Matchstick Mini?

There are so many different floats in the parade, and on one of the floats there is a man dressed up as St. Patrick, with a huge green cloak with a big, huge crown on his head with a big gold chain around his neck with a big, tall stick that looks like a fork.

Matchstick Mini and his little sister love listening to all the different bands going by in the parade and listening to all the different types of music. Some of the bands have twirling sticks, and they throw them high up into the air and catch them. Matchstick Mini loves watching the person at the front of the bands banging on a big drum leading the music bands in the parade.

Even though there are many different types of dancing, Matchstick Mini loves to watch hip-hop dancers the most, with streamers falling from the sky. Matchstick Mini's little sister loves to watch the tap dancers because these are her favorite dancers to watch. Matchstick Mini and his family love looking at the firework display too, and they all look to the sky in amazement at all the different colored fireworks. Matchstick Mini's little sister loves how pretty they look, and she doesn't mind the noise the fireworks make. She knows that noise from fireworks can't hurt you.

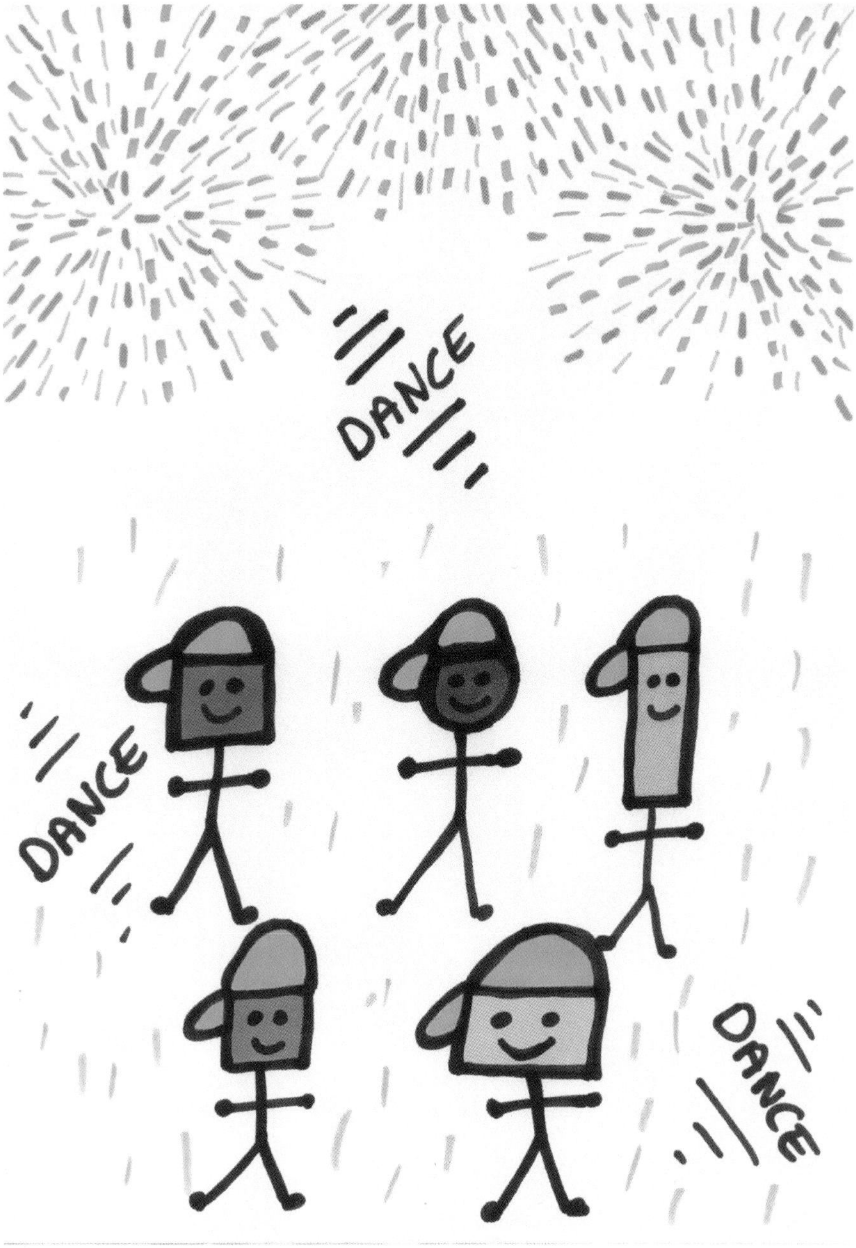
DANCE
DANCE
DANCE

Matchstick Mini gets excited to see the fire brigade taking part in the parade, he knows they have an important job, and he respects firemen for the important work they do. He loves to watch the fire engines going by, and he loves how shiny and red they look. Matchstick Mini thinks the firemen's helmets look cool, and he wonders if he would like to be a fireman in the future someday.

When Matchstick Mini gets home from the parade, he watches the parade on the television, and he is allowed to have some sweets and treats. He only eats sweets and treats on special occasions, and he knows too many sweets are not good for you. Matchstick Mini really enjoyed going to the parade, and he thinks it looks so different watching it on the television because he can see so much more. His family always have a great day at the parade, and they look forward to going again next year.

Before Matchstick Mini goes to bed at night, he likes to draw some of the things he saw that day, he draws flags, bikes, and fireworks. Matchstick Mini is tired when going to bed after having a great St. Patrick's Day, and he dreams about driving a fire engine someday.

Printed in Great Britain
by Amazon

32455746R00021